GREAT MYSTERIES

Vampires

OPPOSING VIEWPOINTS®

Look for these and other exciting *Great Mysteries: Opposing Viewpoints* books:

GREAT MYSTERIES

Vampires

OPPOSING VIEWPOINTS®

by Daniel C. Scavone

Greenhaven Press, Inc.   P.O. Box 289009, San Diego, California 92198-0009

1-98   17.96

Library of Congress Cataloging-in-Publication Data

Scavone, Daniel C., 1934-
    Vampires : opposing viewpoints / by Daniel C. Scavone.
    p. cm. — (Great mysteries)
    Includes bibliographical references and index.
    Summary: Examines the subject of vampires in legend and in history.
    ISBN 0-89908-080-4
    1. Vampires—Juvenile literature. [1.Vampires.] I. Title.
II. Series: Great mysteries (Saint Paul, Minn.)
GR830.V3S28 1990
809'.93375—dc20   90-40131
                                            CIP
                                            AC

*This book is dedicated to my son, Daniel J.,
whose ongoing fascination with the literature of
the mysterious has stimulated my own.*

*A warm thanks for her support, confidence, and endurance
to my editor, Bonnie Szumski*

Contents

Introduction

This book is written for the curious—those who want to explore the mysteries that are everywhere. To be human is to be constantly surrounded by wonderment. How do birds fly? Are ghosts real? Can animals and people communicate? Was King Arthur a real person or a myth? Why did Amelia Earhart disappear? Did history really happen the way we think it did? Where did the world come from? Where is it going?

Great Mysteries: Opposing Viewpoints books are intended to offer the reader an opportunity to explore some of the many mysteries that both trouble and intrigue us. For the span of each book, we want the reader to feel that he or she is a scientist investigating the extinction of the dinosaurs, an archaeologist searching for clues to the origin of the great Egyptian pyramids, a psychic detective testing the existence of ESP.

One thing all mysteries have in common is that there is no ready answer. Often there are *many* answers but none on which even the majority of authorities agrees. *Great Mysteries: Opposing Viewpoints* books introduce the intriguing views of the experts, allowing the reader to participate in their explorations, their theories, and their disagreements as they try to explain the mysteries of our world.

But most readers won't want to stop here. These *Great Mysteries: Opposing Viewpoints* aim to stimulate the reader's curiosity. Although truth is often impossible to discover, the search is fascinating. It is up to the reader to examine the evidence, to decide whether the answer is there—or to explore further.

"Penetrating so many secrets, we cease to believe in the unknowable. But there it sits nevertheless, calmly licking its chops."

H.L. Mencken, American essayist

Prologue

Vampyres issue forth from their graves in the night, attack people sleeping quietly in their beds, suck out all the blood from their bodies and destroy them. . . . Those under the vampyre's fatal influence complain of suffocation and a total weakness of spirit, soon after which they die. Some who, when at the point of death, are asked if they can tell what is causing their debility, reply that some person who recently died has arisen from the tomb to torment them. And when that person is exhumed . . . it appears in all parts fresh and full of blood . . . without corruption. Those who were killed by him become vampyres after their death. To prevent such a spreading evil it is necessary to drive a stake through the body. Blood is seen to flow as if he were alive. Sometimes the vampyre is burnt to ashes, which ends the problem.

These lines were written by Johannes Heinrich Zopfius in his *Dissertation on Serbian Vampyres*, published in 1773. Zopfius's words conjure up the vision we expect when we think about the sinister figure known as the vampire. Such descriptions never fail to thrill and frighten us.

Folklore from all over the world reveals that people in many cultures throughout history have believed in some type of vampire. Many of the an-

(Opposite page) From the movie *Dracula* with actor Bela Lugosi as the famous Transylvanian count.

cient vampires, however, do not resemble the ones we are familiar with from movies and books. Ancient vampires resemble contemporary ones in only two ways: they are dead, restless souls, and they feed on the blood of the living. But ancient vampires do not possess prominent canine teeth or fear garlic, the cross, and the dawn. These are modern touches, added by the writers of horror novels and films to intrigue and scare us.

The main sources that have shaped our modern conception of the vampire are the widely read 1897 novel *Dracula* by Bram Stoker and the Dracula films made famous by actor Bela Lugosi. Lugosi's Dracula character was based on Stoker's novel and was first seen in the 1931 movie *Dracula*. It remains the quintessential image of the vampire.

A Hollywood version of a vampire's victim. Why are vampires the subject of so many horror films?

Lugosi's thick Eastern European accent, prominent fangs, slicked-back black hair, inhumanly pale complexion, and long fingernails have left an unforgettable impression on moviegoers, vampire fans—and nightmare sufferers. Lugosi's Dracula has been imitated and parodied in literally hundreds of movies. The character's influence continues to be seen in such varied works as the 1960s television soap opera series "Dark Shadows," Anne Rice's bestselling series of vampire novels written in the 1980s, and the 1988 teenage thriller movie *The Lost Boys*.

Although in some parts of the world people still hang braids of garlic around their doors and windows to keep vampires away, most people do not believe vampires really exist. Common sense, ordinary daily experiences, and modern science all teach us that there is no such thing.

Still, we read the stories and we watch the movies, and a feeling of fear touches us when an unexpected shadow flits across our consciousness. What can be the reason behind our continued fascination with the vampire? As this book will reveal, there may be many reasons for our ongoing interest in this mysterious and sinister creature.

One

Why Are There So Many Stories About Vampires?

All societies have myths or legends that are passed on from generation to generation. In the United States, the tale of George Washington chopping down the cherry tree and the Brer Rabbit stories are common examples. Myths often relate important information about the culture and people of a particular region or country. For this reason, many experts believe these stories should be studied seriously. The widespread belief in vampires could reveal some interesting information about the people who believe in them.

The Origination of the Vampire

Most very early accounts of vampires are concerned with creatures who suck the blood of the living. Devendra P. Varma, who has traveled extensively in India, Nepal, and Tibet, believes that the Indus River Valley of this region may be where the vampire myth originated. She has found wall paintings and carved figures representing vampire-type gods that date from 3000 B.C. The pictures show vampire-gods with green faces, pale blue bodies, and prominent fangs. The Nepal Lord of Death, for example, holds a skull cup filled with blood and stands on a hill of skeletons in a sea of blood.

(Opposite page) A vampire issues forth from the grave. Why are people fascinated by vampire stories and legends?

People have believed in vampires since the earliest recorded time. Vampire legends date back to the Tibetans, who built monuments like these to protect themselves from evil forces.

Other Indian vampires are the ancient *Rakshasas*. The name means "destroyers." These characters appear in the Vedas, the oldest religious books of the Hindus in India, dating from as early as 1500 B.C.

Hindus also believed in Langsuir, a beautiful woman who died of grief after learning that her baby was born dead. She wears an exquisite green gown. Her long black hair flows down to her ankles. It hides the hole in the back of her neck through which she sucks the blood of babies. In order to stop Langsuir, one must cut her long nails and hair and stuff her locks into the hole in her neck. A woman who dies in childbirth may become like Langsuir unless someone places beads in her mouth, eggs under her armpits, and needles in her palms. These steps prevent her from shrieking, flying, and grasping victims.

Two vampire demons. On the right is the Malay vampire *Penanggalen,* who, according to legend, feeds on the blood of children.

Malaysians believed in a frightful monster-vampire called a *Penanggalen*. One legend says that a woman, startled during her prayers, accidentally kicked herself so hard in the chin that the skin split around her neck and her head became detached from her body. Attached to the head were her stomach and intestines, hanging down in strings. Some say she enters the body of a woman and uses that body to feed on the bodies of children. Others believe that in her hideous form she flies to her victims and seizes them with her teeth as she drains their blood. Malaysians protect themselves by hanging thorny Jeruju leaves at the doors and windows

Many vampire legends incorporate images of dark and brooding castles, such as this one in Romania, as the site of vampirism, murder, and mayhem.

"The origins of the vampire myth lie in the mystery cults of oriental civilizations . . . the Nepalese Lord of Death, the Tibetan Devil, and the Mongolian God of Time."

Dalhousie University professor Devendra P. Varma, *The Vampire in Legend, Lore, and Literature*

"Blood is the key factor in the origins of the vampire myth."

Author Anthony Masters, *The Natural History of the Vampire*

of houses where a child has been born. They believe the Penanggalen will not try to enter their homes for fear of catching her delicate intestines on the prickly leaves.

These and other vampires found in most parts of the world are often believed to seek the blood of babies or young people because it is supposedly more vital and full of energy than that of older people.

These beliefs, all strange and all different, have one thing in common: the fear that powerful creatures can drain the lifeblood of the living. Blood is the essence of life. Loss of blood can cause death. Vampires steal life, supposedly so that their own unnatural lives can continue. Believers in vampires, then, may have thought that drinking blood could bring a person back to life.

An example of this belief is found in Book XVII of the late medieval (1469) epic *Morte d'Arthur*, by Thomas Malory. In the story, Sir Galahad, Sir Percival, and Percival's sister arrive at a castle. A princess who lives in the castle suffers from an ailment for which her physician has prescribed bathing in the blood of a pure maiden. Whenever such a maiden passes by, therefore, the knights of the castle demand a dish full of her blood. Percival's sister, thinking a full dish is not so much, gives her blood and dies. Percival and Galahad then find bodies of many maidens who likewise bled to death for this sick lady. This story incorporates the idea that blood is a medicine or renewal agent that will support life. This idea was common throughout the Middle Ages.

The Chinese Vampire

Chinese tales describe vampires that closely resemble modern ones. This example was reported by G. Willoughby-Meade in *Chinese Ghouls and Goblins* (1928):

> The wife of a man named Liu went in to awaken him from sleep one morning and found his body headless, but with no trace of blood. When she reported this, she was suspected of having murdered Liu herself and was taken into custody. Soon after, a neighbor gathering wood discovered a coffin with its lid partially ajar lying near a neglected grave. Inside was a corpse whose face seemed alive and whose body was covered with white hair. It was holding the missing head of Liu. Its grip was so tight that the arms had to be chopped off in order to release the head. Fresh blood gushed from the arms. The two officials ordered this *kiangshi* [vampire] to be burnt and Liu's widow to be freed.

In Western Europe vampire traditions can be traced back to the Greeks and Romans. Myths from these ancient cultures refer to creatures called

"It might be noted that in some dictionaries, the word 'vampire' is considered to be of Serbian origin."

Belgrade University professor Veselin Cajkanovic, *The Serbian Literary Herald*

"The term vampire is said to be from the Russian *vampir,* which is derived from the root *pi* ('to drink')."

Writer Fred Gettings, *Dictionary of Demons*

Lamiae or *strigoi.* These creatures also drink the blood and eat the flesh of young people.

Two stories tell us about Greek and Roman views of the activities of vampires. About A.D. 22 the traveling teacher Philostratus related a story about a handsome student named Menippus who was about to marry a beautiful and rich woman. Apollonius of Tyana, a wise philosopher, attended the wedding party. Having studied the bride carefully, Apollonius accused her of being a vampire. She finally admitted that, in fact, she was fattening up Menippus so that later she could devour his body. It was her custom, she said, to feed upon young handsome bodies because of their pure red blood.

Philinnion

Another story is told by the Greek writer Phlegon in his book *On Wonders and Giants*, written around A.D. 120. It clearly tells the story of a vampire. Six months after a girl named Philinnion died, she returned to her parents' home to visit Machates, a guest who was using her old room. She came at night and was gone by dawn. She even left him a gold ring and a ribbon that had been buried with her. Convinced by these tokens that their daughter was not really dead, the parents waited in hiding for Philinnion's usual visit to Machates. She came, and joyfully they tried to hug her. But for some reason this caused her only to die again, lying on her old bed. The story spread through the town. People crowded to the house and saw her body. Her tomb was opened, but the slab held only a ring and a cup that Machates had given her on a previous visit. She was not replaced in her vault but burned to ashes outside the city walls. The local priests then performed some rituals to purify the town, but poor Machates killed himself because he had lost his love.

This story reveals that vampires may not always

be deadly. Some seem simply to wish to return to the home they lived in while alive. The motive of love is a fairly common theme in vampire stories. In some cases, a vampire's visit may result in his or her former spouse's death. In others, the vampire simply seeks to enjoy the affectionate companionship he or she had while alive. (Some vampire researchers have argued that the hickey, or "lovebite," is related to the more serious bite of the earnest vampire.) The corpses in these tales returned for a renewal of love. They are not evil. They do not feed off the blood of innocent victims in order to prolong their own grisly lives.

These stories from India, ancient Greece and Rome, medieval England, and China are only a small sample of the thousands of tales of vampires found worldwide. The vampires in them are of many types. All of the tales, however, may reveal some common beliefs or superstitions about the nature of life and death.

For instance, the people in all these cultures knew that life is fragile. Death was feared, and what happened after death was unknown. In addition, the supernatural world seemed filled with dangerous creatures. These powerful creatures from the realm of death could steal the lifeblood of the living. To early people with little of the scientific knowledge we possess today, the vampire may have been a way to account for such things as sudden or unexplained death.

After reading these vampire stories, is it any wonder that people believed in and fear this creature?

Two

How Did Christianity Influence the Belief in Vampires?

In Western and Eastern Europe, belief in vampires was greatly influenced by Christianity. The Catholic church was especially powerful, and its tenets were strictly adhered to by many people throughout Europe. One idea supported by the church was that vampires existed and that they were agents of the devil. The church officially recognized the existence of vampires in 1215, during the Fourth Lateran Council of Catholic Church Leaders in Rome. The church also established itself as the only authority strong enough to eliminate vampires. By recognizing vampires as well as maintaining that church leaders must be present to eliminate them, the church endorsed and reinforced folk beliefs about vampires.

Today it might seem strange that people believed so strongly in vampires and the devil. But in the world of early Christianity (up to A.D. 500) and in all the centuries of the Middle Ages (roughly from 500 to 1600), almost everyone believed in Satan and his demons and vampires.

A story from *History of England* by William of Newburgh (1136-1208) shows the involvement of the church in exterminating vampires. Modern scholars consider William of Newburgh to be a reli-

(Opposite page) The vampire as a devil-like creature. Throughout the Middle Ages, the church strongly believed in Satan, demons, and vampires.

"In physical features, vampires are repulsive: long nails that curve like claws; skin showing a deathly pallor . . . eyes often described as 'dead'; and rat-like fangs designed for attack."

Author Alan Ryan, *Vampires and Other Ghosts*

"The vampire is essentially physically identical to the ordinary human. The vital organs are the same. Many of the body functions are the same."

Professor Feodor Stepanovich Andreiev, Soviet Institute of Esoteric Studies, quoted in *Vampires*

able source of facts, so it is interesting that the following vampire account is included in his history.

According to Newburgh, a certain man died in Buckinghamshire and was buried on the eve of the Ascension in 1196. The following night he suddenly entered his wife's bedroom, causing her the greatest alarm and nearly killing her by leaping upon her with all his weight. He did the same the next night. On the third night she lay awake along with a company of people to watch with her. He still came but was driven away by the crowd. On subsequent nights, he did the same to his own brothers in the same town. The archdeacon then wrote to the bishop of Lincoln to ask his advice in

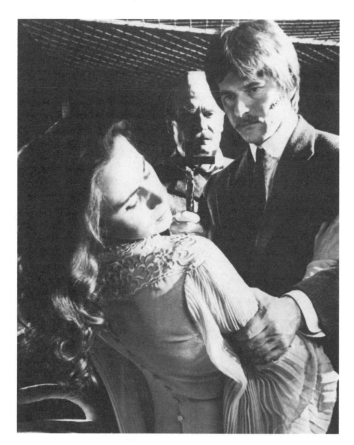

In the 1979 Hollywood version of *Dracula*, a man renders a vampire powerless by flashing a cross in her face.

combatting "so intolerable an evil." The bishop consulted with theologians and learned that similar occurrences had often taken place in England. All agreed that there would be no peace in Buckinghamshire until the body of this poor man was burned to ashes.

The bishop was unwilling to take such drastic action. Instead he wrote out in his own hand an absolution, or pardon from all sins, for this man who had died. The bishop ordered that, regardless of the reason this man wandered from the grave, the archdeacon should open the tomb and lay the pardon upon the breast of the corpse. The body was found uncorrupted, as fresh and undecayed as it had been on the day of the funeral. After the tomb was resealed, the dead man never bothered anyone again. This tale reinforces the idea that only the power of the church could combat vampires.

Another tale from this period shows that vampires feared the power of the church so much that objects considered holy could be used to immobilize

Medieval bishops and clergymen gather in the courtyard of a church. In the Middle Ages, superstitious beliefs of the church provided a fertile ground for vampire legends to flourish.

An abandoned graveyard in France. According to legend, vampires rose from the grave and sought the blood of the living.

"Can the Devil endow a vampire with the qualities of subtility, rarification, increase, and diminishing, so that it may pass through doors and windows? I answer that there is no doubt the Demon can do this."

Vampire researcher and writer Montague Summers, *The Vampire: His Kith and Kin*

"To argue that the devil turns the body of a vampire into a spirit so that it can exit its grave is merely an unverified claim."

Vampire researcher Dom Calmet, quoted in *The Vampire: His Kith and Kin*

them. Walter Map wrote a book called *Anecdotes of the Royal Court* in 1197. It included the story of a knight who had three children. On the morning after each birth, the baby's throat was found slit. Blood stained the cradle. The expected fourth delivery was accompanied by prayers and sacrifice. The house and the surrounding area were brightly lit so that nothing would escape the family's notice or vengeance.

That very day a stranger arrived, tired from his long journey, and begged in the name of God to rest a bit in the castle. He offered to stay up and help watch for the unknown killer of the children. By midnight the members of the household were mysteriously falling asleep. The stranger, however, remained awake and saw the most trusted nurse bend over the cradle, about to slit the infant's throat. Fortunately, the stranger was able to grab her and wake the family. When the nurse would not speak, the stranger charged her with being a vampire who only looked like the real nurse. He pressed the key of the castle chapel to her face. The holy key branded her with its impression. The nurse-vampire flew out of the window howling and screeching and never returned to the castle again. In this story, the key to the chapel, like the cross in other popular tales, scared the vampire away.

In 1489, two Catholic priests, James Sprenger and Henry Kramer, were assigned to write the *Malleus Maleficarum (The Hammer [or Church's Weapon] Against Witches)*, a handbook for use in the Inquisition witch trials. The Inquisition was an official court of the church that tried cases of

During the Inquisition—a medieval court to combat heresy—an accused witch refuses to recant the charges against her. Religious piety during the Middle Ages resulted in the imprisonment, torture, and even death of anyone straying from traditional religious beliefs.

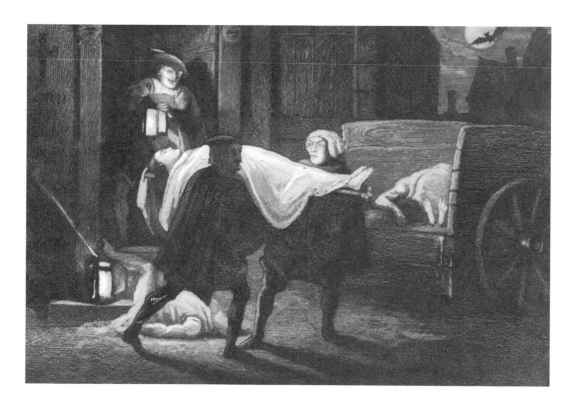

A victim of a plague in 1665 is carried to the "dead cart." Many accounts of vampirism arose during this time because people were unable to explain contagious diseases that wiped out entire communities.

heresy. A heretic was a person who promoted ideas or acted contrary to church teachings.

Some of the activities discussed in the *Malleus Maleficarum* are related to vampirism. One tale included in the book relates the story of a certain town where many people were dying of a plague. A rumor circulated that the plague was being caused by a certain woman who had died and now was slowly eating her burial shroud. The villagers believed that the plague would not end until she had digested the whole shroud. A town council decided to dig up the body. They indeed found the shroud half eaten. Struck with horror, the mayor immediately cut off her head with his sword. The plague stopped. The *Malleus* is filled with similar accounts. All of them reveal how seriously the church regarded vampires.

The Greek Orthodox church provided another powerful connection between the church and vampirism. The Greek Orthodox tradition has always expected from its members complete obedience, conformity, and attendance. Failure to follow these standards would put a member in danger of excommunication, being expelled from the church. The church charged that if a sinner was excommunicated, he or she was more prone to vampirism. This was because excommunication supposedly stopped the body from decomposing after death and prevented the spirit from finding eternal rest in heaven. Favorite curses among the Greeks are, "May the earth not receive him" and "May he remain incorrupt." Again, the power of the church is evident. Nonbelievers or sinners could be doomed to roam the earth as vampires for not following the church's teachings.

Vatican City in Rome—the center of the Roman Catholic church that is ruled by the pope. Here, in the seventeenth century theologian Leo Allatius studied vampirism and other supernatural phenomena.

Tombstones line a beach on an island in Ireland. Leo Allatius believed accounts that the dead rose from tombs such as these in the darkness of night, seeking a feast of blood.

Among the important students of vampires was the Greek scholar, physician, and theologian Leo Allatius. During his long career, he spent many years studying in the archives of the Vatican Library in Rome and working as a missionary in Europe for various popes. He died in Rome in 1669. His study of vampires appeared in his book, *On the Current Opinions of Certain Greeks*, published in 1645:

> The *vrykolakas* [the Greek word for vampire] is the body of an evil and wicked man, often one who has been excommunicated. Such bodies do not, like other corpses, decompose after burial, but having a very tough skin, become swollen and distended. . . . The skin becomes stretched like the parchment of a drum.

These bodies, Allatius continued, are controlled by the devil and come out of their tombs at night. They knock on doors of houses, calling residents by name. Anyone who answers will die the next day. Since people know that the vrykolakas never calls a name twice, they always wait to hear it a second time. If people begin to die without explanation, graves of the recently dead are opened. If a body is found uncorrupted, the priests are summoned to perform services, and it is burned on a pile of dry wood.

Allatius firmly believed in vampires. He wrote, "It is stupid not to admit that such bodies are frequently found incorrupt in their graves. God may, indeed, permit the devil to do his worst."

The church often encouraged these beliefs in order to entice people to obey and fear the church. In addition, among peasants who could neither read nor write, the church was the primary source of information about the world. The belief in vampires flourished alongside the belief in Christianity. But other reasons also reinforced the acceptance of vampires. In order to understand these, it is important to examine the way of life in the Middle Ages.

Three

What Other Factors Influenced Vampire Beliefs?

(Opposite page) During the Black Death—the epidemic of the bubonic plague that swept across Europe in the fourteenth century—belief in vampirism flourished. Many victims, like this mother and sick child, thought that supernatural culprits were responsible for the great suffering and death.

Accounts of vampirism became common in Europe in the fourteenth century. In 1348 the Black Death, the worst outbreak of the bubonic plague, began its spread across Europe. It surged and retreated for the next three hundred years, wiping out whole villages. Between 1347 and 1350, approximately twenty-five million people died from this terrible disease. There was scarcely a family that did not lose at least one member, and most families lost several.

Completely perplexed and not knowing its cause or its treatment, people everywhere formed notions of what was behind the plague. Historians are unsure why, but vampires were thought to be a major culprit. Even church and town officials could not reverse the popular demand that graves be opened and that any vampire be found and destroyed.

Victims of the plague who gradually wasted away and died were thought to have been visited by a dead relative or enemy. In these cases, the person in the village who had died most recently under extraordinary circumstances—such as murder, suicide, accident, or at too early an age—would be the suspected vampire. If that person had some relationship with the earliest victims of the epidemic,

the suspicion increased. And if these first victims had mentioned seeing this relative or enemy in dreams during their last illness, the case was confirmed. Village authorities, in the presence of a priest, would exhume, or dig up, the body of the suspected vampire and perform the local version of killing the undead corpse.

If that did not end the epidemic, then the search continued by exhuming the bodies of other recently dead people. Finally, if all these efforts failed, a white horse or a black horse, ridden by a young virgin boy or girl, would be led over the graves in the local cemetery. If a grave contained a vampire, the horse would refuse to step over it.

These fervent beliefs were fueled by ignorance. Until the twentieth century, most people around the world had little formal education and could neither read nor write. Without the knowledge gained from reading or education, it is almost impossible for people to evaluate sensibly common superstitions and fears. To such people, any story can seem true, especially if an authority figure such as a parent, teacher, doctor, or minister tells it.

Little Scientific Knowledge

Even the few people living in these times who could read and write had little scientific knowledge. During this time, little was known about medicine or the physical world. For example, as recently as the seventeenth century, doctors did not know how diseases spread. Not until the invention of the microscope around 1600 did people begin to know about germs and bacteria. In the absence of scientific data, people held many fantastical beliefs about how and why diseases spread. One such belief was that vampires were responsible for epidemics or plagues. People believed that vampires sought revenge upon the living by inflicting these diseases.

Another story from the *History of England* by

A doctor visits a plague victim. Doctors of the Middle Ages possessed little scientific knowledge and could not explain or control the diseases that spread through entire populations.

A tomb in England—the alleged home of an eighteenth-century vampire. What accounts for the richness and diversity of vampire tales that have survived throughout the ages?

William of Newburgh gives an official account of how a vampire could cause a plague. A wealthy squire who lived in Berwick-on-Tweed in northern England died and became a bloodsucking creature known as the Berwick Vampire. At night he would exit his tomb and wander the streets, causing dogs to howl and yelp. The air became foul from his decomposing body, which caused a plague. "There was hardly a house which did not mourn its dead," according to Newburgh. The town became virtually deserted. Finally, the young men of the town decided to exhume the corpse, hack it to pieces, and burn it to ashes. The plague, however, returned, wiping out most of the townspeople.

Historians thus believe the Black Death and other plagues may have influenced vampire beliefs. Another factor that seems to influence cultural belief in vampires is geographic location. For obscure reasons, Eastern Europe seems to be an area rich in vampire mythology.

Bram Stoker, author of *Dracula*, the best-known novel about vampires, set his tale in the Carpathian

A map of Eastern Europe. Vampire stories of today are rooted in the supernatural lore of the Eastern Europeans.

Mountains of Transylvania, "the land beyond the forest." It was a fitting choice. This area is currently part of Romania, one of the countries of Eastern Europe, which also encompasses Greece, Albania, Bulgaria, Yugoslavia, Hungary, and the Soviet Union. Here, most people are peasant farmers or craftspeople. In terms of urbanization and industrialization, these countries lag far behind the rest of Europe. People live by their beliefs and by the time-honored customs and rituals of their forefathers. The belief in the vampire has always been strong among these Slavic peoples.

In *Dracula*, Stoker warns the reader about the Eve of St. George's Day, May 3. On this night, the forces of evil, including vampires, have complete sway over the earth. In the novel, Stoker has faithfully reflected an actual belief widely held by people throughout Eastern Europe. Another crucial day was St. Andrew's Eve, November 29. On both of these nights, people should not be out for any reason. Doors, windows, chimneys, keyholes, and livestock should be rubbed with garlic to keep out vampires and other evil forces.

In the beliefs of Eastern Europeans, there are numerous ways people can become vampires. Although stories rarely report that a vampire's bite will turn the victim into a vampire as well, one Greek monk's account from 1888 does assert that the bite "makes its victims like itself, so that it gathers about it an ever larger train of followers." In addition, sinful acts such as murder, perjury, or suicide might cause someone to become a vampire.

Innocent people, too, could become vampires. A murder victim might return as a vampire seeking re-

The Carpathian Mountains—setting of Bram Stoker's *Dracula*.

A Romanian peasant woman pauses before a graveyard. Many Slavic people are still haunted by the belief that apparitions and vampires rise from their graves at nightfall.

venge. Someone who died young might return as a vampire to somehow extend his or her life. In Bulgaria, a person born with a harelip (a split in the upper lip) or with only one nostril was thought to be a likely vampire. In Greece, where most people have brown eyes and dark hair, a person with blue eyes or red hair was thought likely to become a vampire after death. In Romania, the seventh son of a seventh son was a vampire prospect. These cases seem to point to a general rule: people tended to believe that anyone who was somehow different was a potential vampire. In northern climates, where most people are blond and fair, a swarthy person may be suspect. In the south, just the opposite is the case.

In some places it was forbidden to eat the meat of a sheep that had been killed by a wolf for fear that the person would become a vampire. In Romania and Bulgaria people also believed a person might become a vampire if he or she was born or died during the twelve "unclean" days between Christmas and January 6, Epiphany.

The following nineteenth-century account from Bulgaria reveals other aspects of vampire folklore.

Fervent Beliefs

A couple was married for thirty years. During all those years, the husband was always absent from home at night. In their neighborhood, animals frequently died mysteriously, completely drained of their blood. Finally, people connected the wife's complaints to the animal deaths, and the man came under suspicion. When he was found to have only one nostril, the villagers were convinced that he was a vampire. They formed a mob and burned the man alive.

A widespread belief in Eastern European folklore is that a dead person may become a vampire if during his wake, visitation, or funeral a cat jumps over his coffin. In other versions, the cat is replaced by a hen. Friends and relatives are stationed to watch over the coffin at all times until burial. Imagine what dread dreams would visit a person who had fallen asleep during his watch and allowed another vampire to come into existence. He or she would live in fear that the vampire would certainly seek revenge for such carelessness.

In Greek accounts of returning corpses, there is very little, if any, bloodsucking. Greek vampires apparently returned for love or mischief. About 1700, a French botanist, Pitton de Tournefort, was on the Greek Island of Mykonos when a peasant was murdered. Two days after burial, the peasant was reportedly seen walking at night. He entered houses where he "turned over furniture, put out lights, hugged people from behind, and played many roguish tricks."

At first people laughed, but when religious services could not stop his activities, the priests ordered his body removed from the grave. The old town butcher was ordered to remove the heart, which he looked for in the peasant's belly until someone suggested higher up. All applauded when

"The vrykolakas is the body of a man of a wicked and debauched life, very often one who has been excommunicated by his bishop."

Vampire researcher and theologian Leo Allatius, quoted in *The Vampire: His Kith and Kin*

"In places like Sicily and Greece where the law of the vendetta ruled for so long, a murdered man whose death went unavenged would rise up as a vampire."

Author Douglas Hill, *Man, Myth, and Magic*

A family of Bulgarian peasants. Does fact or fiction dominate their tales of alleged vampirism?

he located and removed it. Incense was burned to cover the great stench of the body. The butcher remarked on the warmth of the corpse. Those who stood near the body noted that the blood was still red and the body was lifelike, not stiff. They passed these observations to the crowd and the word *vrykolakas* was on everyone's lips.

Tournefort remarked, "We scientists could see that the 'red blood' was nothing but a bad-smelling slime." Finally, since the mischief continued even

A group of citizens drives a stake through the heart of a suspected vampire.

after the heart had been burned, the entire body was again exhumed and burned on a pyre covered with tar. The complaints of the vampire's activities ceased after that. Meanwhile, some mischief-makers were discovered who, Tournefort added, were likely to be the cause of the vampire scare.

Not Everyone Believed in Vampires

As this anecdote hints, not everyone in the eighteenth and nineteenth centuries believed in vampires. Some tried to educate people and prove that vampires were not real. One of these was the French priest Dom August Calmet (1672-1757). Calmet wrote a book called *A Treatise on Apparitions, Spirits and Vampires*, which was published in 1746.

He noted that, curiously, vampires seemed particularly to infest Slavic countries. They did not appear in Western Europe, he said, until the 1680s, during his own lifetime. He also said that fads of a supernatural type seemed to come and go in cycles. Sometimes it was a witch craze, but

> recently for about the last sixty years, we have been witnesses of new extraordinary incidents in Hungary, Moravia, Silesia, Poland. In those places, we are told, men dead for several months return from the tomb, speak, walk about in hamlets and villages, and injure men and beasts, whose blood they drain, causing illness and death. The only cure for these horrible attacks is to dig up the corpses, drive a sharp stake through the bodies, cut off the heads, tear out the hearts, or burn the bodies to ashes. The name of these ghosts is Oupires or Vampires, which in the Slavonic languages means bloodsuckers. The details of actual cases are so well-attested and legally documented that it seems impossible not to accept them.

Calmet seriously wondered about whether vampires existed. He instinctively thought that there was no such thing: "For my part I think the whole

"In danger of becoming vrykolakas are those who have not been buried, who have been cursed . . . murdered, who have killed themselves . . . who have been evil . . . and those who are polluted."

Author Eva Blum, *The Dangerous Hour*

"There are several different ways to become a vampire. The usual way is, of course, to be bitten by one and have him drink your blood."

Author Thomas Aylesworth, *Vampires and Other Ghosts*

Sixteenth-century woodcuts (right and below) illustrate ancient medical practices. Although many of these practices killed the people they sought to cure, people continued to attribute death and disease to vampirism.

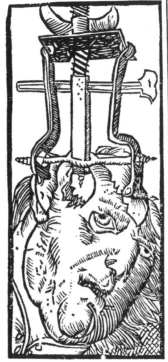

history vain and utterly without foundation. The more absurd and contradictory are the various tales which were told, the more strongly am I confirmed in my opinion."

His first notion, as a scholar, was that reputed vampires were really people who had been buried alive. Still, he adds, "The study is useful and for the good of religion. For if vampires truly return from their graves, then it is necessary to prove it; if not true, then vampirism must be exposed as error and illusion." This quote illustrates that Calmet, like scientists and scholars today, insisted on proof before he believed an opinion or conclusion. By questioning what these people saw when they uncovered the grave of the "vampire," Calmet was rationally examining the evidence, much as a modern scientist would.

Calmet was rare in his ability to break out of the

folk beliefs and superstitions that surrounded him. Calmet questioned the very details of vampire appearances that would puzzle us today. Why, he wondered, were vampires appearing mainly in Eastern Europe, where people were especially superstitious? He explained away the redness of the vampire's blood and the flexibility of their limbs as a result of sudden death, "well known by physicians." Again, Calmet's thoughts on vampires are remarkably scientific and modern for his period.

Dom Calmet was troubled by some of the puzzling contradictions in the vampire accounts that he researched. He wondered how a vampire could leave its grave and return without disturbing the earth, since the vampire has a tangible, physical body that does physical harm. Or, once out, why did

Many people believed that vampires changed into bats, thus gaining the mobility to spread the plague west.

it return to the grave? If it is not the actual corpse that stirs from the grave, but only a spirit that appears to the living, what is it that brings life to the spirit? Calmet concluded, "The stories told of these apparitions, and all the distress caused by these supposed vampires, are totally without solid proof. I am not surprised that the Sorbonne [a university in Paris] has condemned the outrages—decapitation, staking, or burning—inflicted on these innocent corpses. It is astonishing that the magistrates and secular bodies have not used their legal authority to

Eighteenth-century men bury victims of a plague in a mass grave.

put an end to it. This is a mysterious and difficult matter, and I leave bolder and more proficient minds to resolve it."

But the books of Calmet and others like him did not stop the belief in vampirism. Between 1690 and 1725, the superstition spread throughout Europe. French and Dutch news journals reported vampire epidemics in France, Serbia, Hungary, and Greece. The Hungarian vampire epidemic was the topic of dozens of learned dissertations in Germany in the 1720s and 1730s. During these decades disease epidemics killed many people. Does this mean that vampires are purely mythic inventions used to provide an explanation for plague and disease and other strange occurrences? The answer is probably yes. Medieval people were hampered not only by their ignorance but by traditions and beliefs that went unquestioned. This is not surprising, really, because they had no scientific knowledge to replace these beliefs.

It is still true in modern times that when knowledge is not available, superstition often prevails. For example, until the actual cause of and a cure for cancer is found, there are many beliefs that circulate explaining how it is caused and how to cure it. People today believe in some medical cures but may also believe that positive thinking, natural food, and other remedies work as well. It is impossible to say whether they do or not. This willingness to accept unproven answers was true of medieval people as well. Without proof of what caused the diseases, unexplained deaths, and other violent happenings that plagued their lives, these people accepted vampires as a reasonable explanation.

A woodcut of medieval chemists at work. Some scientists, like Dom Calmet, attempted to discount popular folk beliefs and superstitions characteristic of the Middle Ages.

Four

How Were Vampires Destroyed?

The people of each region of Europe have their own version of how to destroy a vampire. In some accounts, vampires are destroyed when someone drives a stake through its heart. There are also versions in which a specific type of wood is needed. In Romania, only a hawthorn stake cannot be pulled out by the vampire. In other versions, the stake could be a red-hot iron poker.

In some versions, the vampire's head must be removed and placed between the knees of the corpse. Other accounts call for the decapitation *and* the stake. In Romania people may insert forks in the eyes of the dead person who is thought to be a vampire. Gypsies of Eastern Europe believe that a long pole thrust into the ground above the coffin is sufficient. If a vampire should try to leave its grave, he or she would be impaled by the pole. This method eliminates the need to exhume the body.

In different accounts, the head, heart, or entire body is burned. This may be in addition to staking. After cremation, the ashes are carefully reburied, or sometimes they are strewn in a river because some people believe that vampires cannot cross running water.

Why were there so many ways to destroy a

(Opposite page) A picture from *Varney the Vampire*, in which soldiers discover a desecrated corpse. A stake through the heart of a corpse was a popular method of killing vampires.

vampire? The answer seems to be in the very nature of folklore. Many people contributed ideas on how to kill a vampire, some of which stuck after they were tried and found to work.

Preventing Vampires' Progress

As a general rule, cremation of the entire body is the surest means of finally ending the vampire's career. As one reads the case studies of reputed vampires, it is obvious that all other measures merely prevent the vampire from leaving the grave or render the vampire harmless if it does exit. These methods do not destroy the vampire. Vampires are sometimes buried face downward at a crossroad, for example. If a vampire is buried face down, its efforts to dig its way out will only put it deeper in the ground. If it does manage to reverse direction, leaves the grave, and finds itself at a crossroad, the vampire will then encounter the difficulty of selecting a direction.

A vampire may be buried with its mouth stuffed with garlic, nails, or thorns to prevent its biting someone. Sometimes the grave site is strung around with thorny bushes to snag the vampire's clothing, thus slowing it down when it tries to leave the grave. A cross may be placed upon the grave to prevent its exit. Often, millet or corn is scattered over the suspected vampire's body. Popular legend maintains that the vampire must eat and/or count every grain before it can exit its coffin.

These methods prevent the vampire's progress, but do not destroy it. But if cremation kills a vampire, why were these other efforts made? Why did people not exhume the body or discover it by day in its coffin and burn it? The answer seems to be that total cremation is not as easy as it seems. The amount of wood or other fuel required is immense and costly—about fifteen hundred pounds of coal. The fire must reach and stay at sixteen hundred

Some medieval people believed that a cross on the grave prevented unquiet corpses from leaving their coffins.

degrees Fahrenheit for one hour. The body must be wrapped in animal fat to promote burning. Complete destruction of a body is difficult to achieve.

These other steps designed to hamper the activities of vampires are much less expensive. Two case studies reported by Agnes Murgoci in 1927 describe other ways to ward off a vampire.

According to Murgoci's report, in 1899 in a village of Romania, old Mrs. Gheorghita died. After a few months, her grandchildren began to die one by one. Her sons, full of local superstitions about the undead, dug up her body, cut it in two, and reburied it. Still, other relatives died. Again they exhumed her body and found it still intact. This time they removed her heart, which bled freely. They cut it in four pieces and burned it on hot cinders. They mixed the ashes in water and made the remaining children drink the mixture. This ended the mysterious deaths. After this incident, it was believed that drinking water plus the ashes of a vampire would eliminate the vampire.

An undated account describes the plight of a man from Transylvania named Dimitriou Vaideanu. Each of his children died shortly after birth. Certain that it was the doing of a *vampir*, he and his neighbors decided to take a white horse to the cemetery and lead it over the graves of his wife's relations. Sure enough, the horse refused to step over the grave of Joana Marta, the wife's mother. It stood there neighing and snorting and beating its hooves.

In the eighteenth century, undertakers exhume the corpses of suspected vampires.

When they uncovered Joana's body, she sat straight up as if alive. Dimitriou ended the nightmare of the dying infants by burning his wife's mother.

A corpse is burned on a funeral pyre. Some people believed that this would prevent the deceased from becoming a vampire.

Vampire Beliefs Persist

In 1940 Gordon Cooper wrote a book about burial practices around the world. It was entitled *I Searched the World for Death*. In it he relates how he was invited to witness a Bulgarian ceremony known as the "second burial." This ritual is still performed today to prevent the deceased from becoming a vampire. Cooper's host told him that five years ago, a man had died during the "Unclean Days when the world is ruled by the forces of evil." The deceased himself had made his family promise him this second burial. It was, in any case, a fairly common ritual. As evening approached, everybody went to the churchyard. The sexton sprinkled holy water on each member of the group. Men and women divided into groups on either side of the grave. The priest appeared with a cross, a lighted candle, and a spade. After a prayer, the grave was opened. It was just an overgrown mound and a wooden cross. The bones were lifted out and placed on a sheet. After more prayers, the bones and skull were washed with wine and put into a bag. Oil and wine were poured into the grave, the bones were replaced, and the grave was refilled. No one needed to fear this poor soul. He would not become a vampire.

In his book *The Burial Rituals of Rural Greece*, Loring Danforth relates that in present-day Greece examination and reburial of the dead is the usual custom after a prescribed number of years. In fact, graves are rented for the period and normally are not family-owned. After the unearthing, the family and friends ritually cleanse the bones, recite

A graveyard in Ireland. In Greece, corpses were buried, exhumed, and then buried again. This custom ensured family members that the body was decomposing and was not a vampire.

prayers, and collect the bones in a clean sack. In a second burial, then, they place the sack in the common mortuary house at one end of the cemetery. The whole procedure is based on a confused set of religious and superstitious ideas that date back to the folklore of the Greek Orthodox tradition, likely formed during the times of the black death. The most important element in the ritual is surely the need to observe the body to ensure that it is properly decomposing and is not a vampire. In Romania, too, the second burial is a common practice in many districts.

Another account of Greek beliefs comes from an interview Cooper had with a Greek-American in 1934. "They say that once a vrykolakas married and even begot two children. But every Saturday his wife would miss him. . . . Once at a party people noticed that his singing voice sounded like that of a man who had died. . . . So the villagers made plans, because we are told that the vrykolakas does not come out on Saturday. They opened the grave of the man who had died and found the husband inside. He begged for mercy, not to be burned. But they showed him no mercy."

These accounts present some of the reasons for the widespread belief in vampires. And this belief reaches into the twentieth century.

What do these anecdotes mean? Why do they exist? What type of phenomena are they describing? There are many possibilities.

"It is thought that a vampire, if prowling out of his tomb at night, may be shot and killed with a silver bullet that has been blessed by a priest."

Vampire researcher and writer Montague Summers, *The Vampire: His Kith and Kin*

"The vampire will exist up until the least bit of his body exists."

Belgrade University professor Veselin Cajkanovic, *The Serbian Literary Herald*

Five

How Can Vampires Be Explained?

Belief in vampires was originally the result of and has continued to be nourished by certain facts. For example, a dead body appears pale or even gray because the blood collects in the back of the body. The sight of such a body might easily suggest a body drained of blood, the work of vampires, to people who do not know the physical reason for the paleness. There are many other natural and scientific factors that have contributed to the belief in vampires.

Catalepsy

Catalepsy is suspended animation. It is the state of a person who is alive but whose breathing, pulse, and other vital signs have slowed down so much that the person seems dead, even to trained doctors. This condition is probably the result of a disorder of the nervous system. Catalepsy is not permanent. Cataleptics can see and hear but cannot move even an eyelash. Imagine the trauma of hearing yourself pronounced dead, of sensing the earth shoveled on your coffin, of coming out of catalepsy and gasping for breath as you attempt to claw your way out of the confinement of your coffin.

Montague Summers, one of the most important

(Opposite page) A corpse waves its arms from the confines of a coffin. Such occurrences have been reported throughout history.

The painting *Buried Alive*, by Antoine Wiertz depicts a woman's horrifying experience with premature burial.

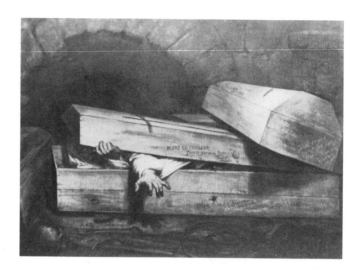

students of supernatural phenomena, noted that statistics in the United States from the early twentieth century record as many as fifty known cases of premature burial each year. In modern times, it has become the law in most places that dead bodies must be embalmed before burial. The embalming, which is done by undertakers, replaces blood with preserving fluids that prevent decay. Catalepsy is thus no longer a problem: if a person is not really dead but merely cataleptic, after embalming he or she is certainly dead.

Through most of history, the dead were buried without embalming. If a person was in a cataleptic trance, he or she might be buried alive. This was no doubt one reason for the widespread custom of holding a one- or two-day wake before burial. People still hold wakes or visitations today, though the original reason is not known to many people.

Since exhumation was quite common because of belief in vampires, we must suppose that an occasional cataleptic was exhumed. Moreover, grave diggers probably heard once in a while some groan or other sound coming from a recent grave. In these cases, what the examiners saw upon opening the box or casket must have been horrifying. The hands would be bloody from the futile, frantic attempts of the person to scratch his or her way to freedom. The blood-spattered face would be contorted in the expression of one practically scared to death and finally dead by suffocation. Here, everyone would agree, was surely a vampire. The blood, they would say, was that of its latest victim.

In 1851 Dr. Herbert Mayo published his book *On the Truths Contained in Popular Superstitions.* He was convinced that "bodies found in the so-called Vampyr state . . . were the bodies of persons who had been buried alive." Other factors in "Vampyr superstition" troubled him, however. He puzzled over why people who believed they had been visited by a vampire often fell into a deathlike trance. He finally concluded that people of weak

Men exhume the victim of a premature burial. They will examine the corpse for evidence of vampirism.

disposition could be strongly affected by their dreams. The dream of a vampire visit could result in a powerful conviction that the visit had really occurred. Such impressionable people might indeed fall into a death-trance, coma, or cataleptic state. In Eastern European communities where the vampire cult was strong, the problem could become epidemic.

Yet Mayo could not convince himself that his explanation was the correct one. He wrote, "To myself, I must confess, this explanation, the best I am in a position to offer, appears barren."

Thus Mayo, like many before him, remained puzzled by the sheer weight of the evidence—the many eyewitness accounts, stories, and examples. He found his explanation lacking and was gnawed by some nagging doubt that perhaps no scientific explanation was adequate to explain vampires.

Porphyria

In the last five years, medical explanations have been offered that account for both vampire and werewolf beliefs. A leading theory states that supposed vampires and werewolves may have been suffering from a rare hereditary blood disease known as porphyria. Porphyria is characterized by the inability of the body to produce *heme*, a component of hemoglobin, which is a major component of red blood. Today there are effective treatments for porphyria, such as the injection of healthy blood heme. Without treatment, however, the porphyria sufferer could have horrible symptoms, such as extreme sensitivity to sunlight, which can cause sores and scars on the skin and excessive hairiness. In severe cases, the fingers and nose sometimes fall off. The skin of the gums and lips might tighten and stretch, causing the teeth to appear very prominent and fanglike.

Porphyriacs would avoid sunlight because of

Can porphyria—a disease often resulting in a craving for blood—explain apparent vampire activity?

Actor Lon Chaney in full make-up for a werewolf role. The excessive hairiness of werewolf-like creatures may have been the result of porphyria, before medical treatment for the disease became available.

their sensitivity, probably coming out only at night. If they were seen, they were probably a horrible sight. Hairy and repulsive, they might suck the blood of some small animal or of someone close to them. Without knowing why they had the urge to do this, porphyriacs were driven in a desperate attempt to acquire the heme their bodies could not generate.

Porphyria is hereditary. In some cases relatives have been bitten for their blood simply because they were handy when the porphyria sufferer needed an immediate supply. These victims might later show the same porphyria symptoms and seem to become vampires as the result of having been bitten by one. The truth is that they had already acquired porphyria at birth, since the disease is hereditary.

Moreover, in earlier times when travel was less common and inbreeding more common, the heredity factor played a larger role. The occurrence of the

A movie still from the famous 1922 film *Nosferatu*. This film set the stage for future vampire films.

disease in many members of a community might well have fostered a belief in the transmission of vampirism from one person to another in a certain village or community.

Oddly, garlic, which stimulates heme production in healthy people, contains a chemical that worsens the painful symptoms of porphyria. Wearing garlic would therefore protect someone from being attacked by a porphyriac. The poor porphyriac would avoid any contact with garlic because it caused pain, not because he or she was a vampire. This bit of folklore—that garlic can protect one from a vampire—apparently may have some basis in scientific fact. This theory was first introduced in 1985 by Dr. David Dolphin of the University of British Columbia in Vancouver, Canada.

The Vampire as Astral Body Projection

Scott Rogo, writing in *Fate* magazine (1965), which is devoted to occult subjects, suggests that vampires do exist. They are not, however, physical beings or always evil, Rogo stresses. He offers an interpretation that fits very well some of the documented descriptions of vampire activity.

Rogo is a parapsychologist, a person who studies occult and psychic phenomena. He believes that every living thing has a spiritual "astral body" that can actually be projected outside the physical body. He cites the work of the French psychic, Z.T. Pierart, who wrote that vampires may be the astral bodies of people prematurely buried. The astral body acts instinctively, not rationally. It leaves the physical body to "vampirize" living things of their vitality in order to nourish itself.

Franz Hartmann, a Viennese physician and psychic, agrees and traces the idea of the astral body to the Renaissance chemist, Paracelsus (1493-1541). Hartmann thinks that someone who is dead may project an astral body that can materialize and live an apparently normal life, as some vampire accounts relate, by draining life energy from the living.

A striking example is the case of nineteenth-century Mollie Fancher. She was blind and crippled and lived under medical observation for years without eating any substantial food. But animals brought into her presence died almost immediately without being maltreated in any way. Was this a case, Hartmann asked, of her astral projection drawing off nourishment from the animals in order to keep Mollie alive?

The Vampire as Bloodthirsty Mass Murderer

History has recorded cases of individuals who craved human blood for one reason or another. Their murder trials are well-documented with the

In films, stories, and books, the vampire is portrayed as a bloodthirsty, evil spirit that preys on innocent victims, such as this sleeping female.

testimony of witnesses. These blood-seekers were not corpses. They were living people, but their abnormal bloody activities may have caused people to believe they were vampires.

One of the most famous examples is Vlad Dracula (1431-1476) of Romania, the inspiration for Bram Stoker's novel *Dracula*. Vlad spent the greater part of his life defending his lands and his people's Christian religion against the Ottoman Turks. Dracula is honored as a Christian warrior and is considered a great patriot by the people of Romania. There was, however, another side to the man.

In 1458 Dracula raided the Romanian town of Brasov, impaling hundreds of German citizens on top of St. Jacob's Hill. He became known as the Impaler because this was his favorite method of execution.

Around 1470 in Frankfurt and elsewhere in Germany, pamphlets contained accounts of the Brasov raid with a drawing of Dracula dining amid

Romanian history is filled with accounts of vampirism and supernatural phenomena. Today, many Romanians practice religious piety as a form of protection against evil forces.

the stakes of his impaled victims and the headless bodies at his feet. He seems to be feasting on human flesh and blood. This picture may be one reason he became associated with Romanian vampire legends.

German and Russian pamphlets recall Dracula's cruelty to Saxons residing in his lands. They show him as a demented psychopath. One manuscript even refers to him as a vampire. Since his cruelty is emphasized by many different people, scholars assume that it is true.

Dracula and Cannibalism

Two anecdotes emphasize Dracula's fascination with cannibalism. In one, some three hundred Mogul Tartars strayed into Dracula's territory. Dracula took the three best men among them and had them fried. The others were made to eat them. Dracula then said, "You will eat each other in the same way unless you go fight the Turks." The Tartars were happy to go and fight the Turks.

In the second story, Dracula caught a gypsy who had stolen. Other gypsies came to beg his freedom. Dracula ordered them to hang the thief, but they said it was not their custom. Dracula then had the gypsy boiled in a pot, and when he was cooked, Dracula forced the others to eat him, flesh and bone.

Was Dracula a vampire? If vampires were living, breathing, bloodthirsty mass murderers, perhaps he was. It is certainly true that his name and the concept of the vampire were joined together first and forever in the mind of Bram Stoker. Curiously, when archaeologists opened Dracula's grave in 1931, he was not in it.

The strange and horrifying story of Countess Elisabeth Bathory (1560-1614) is another example of a murderer whose activities resemble those of a vampire. This countess lived in the Csejthe Castle

This plaque is located at the birthplace of Count Dracula, in the preserved fifteenth-century town Sighisoara in Romania.

in the Carpathian Mountains of Hungary. Her marriage was one of the great society events of the day. Even the Hapsburg emperor Maximilian II attended. Her trial was equally huge, and her notoriety spread among the nobility.

As the story goes, once when Elisabeth slapped her maid, her face was stained from the girl's bloody nose. Wiping off the blood, she noticed that her complexion seemed fresher. This set off a series of horrible crimes that became fully known only during Elisabeth's trial in 1611. Determined to keep her whole body looking young and fresh, she regularly took baths in the blood drained from the bodies of young girls murdered in her own castle. She would lure them there with promises of employment. Poor, older widows in neighboring towns were paid well to procure the girls.

As unbelievable as this story seems, it was taken directly from the statements of her maids at

The castle built by Vlad Dracula, on whom the character Count Dracula is based.

Elisabeth's trial. The raid of the castle by the authorities discovered several girls in different stages of torture. In the main hall lay a girl, dead and drained of blood. A list found in Elisabeth's desk, written in her own hand, put the number of her victims at 650. Their bodies were disposed of in various cemeteries and in the castle dungeons. Elisabeth was found guilty and sentenced to life imprisonment in her bedroom. All the doors of her bedroom were walled up, with only a small opening for food to be passed through. She lived nearly four years in this condition.

Acceptance of Vampires

Well-publicized cases such as this one would encourage the widespread acceptance of vampires. The following cases had the same impact.

The figure dubbed in the French press in 1883 as the "Monster of Montluel" was in reality two fiendish people, a young man named Martin Dummolard and an older, dominating woman named Justine Lafayette. Lafayette had perverse control over the young man and ordered him to kill a fifteen-year-old girl. Dummolard killed her by ripping open her throat and draining her body of its blood. He also mutilated the corpse. This was the first of eighty nearly identical murders in five years. After a sensational trial in 1888, Lafayette was beheaded by the guillotine, and Dummolard was imprisoned in an asylum.

Fritz Haarmann was known as the "Hanover Vampire" at his trial in 1924. He ran a butcher shop with a cooked-food deli counter in Hanover, Germany. Haarmann would linger in railway stations, befriend young men between twelve and eighteen years old, and invite them to his rooms. After serving them a fine meal, he would bite their throats until they died. He then sliced the tenderest parts of their bodies and sold the flesh at his deli

A vampire springs upon his prey in *Varney the Vampire*—the vampire book that preceeded Bram Stoker's *Dracula*.

counter, sometimes as sausages. All this came out at his notorious trial, at which at least twenty-four victims were counted.

In 1931 Peter Kurten, the "Monster of Dusseldorf," was brought to trial. A journalist covering the case reported, "The most extraordinary and horrible point about Kurten's nocturnal prowling lay in its association with the vampire and werewolf of ancient tradition. It was his habit and principal satisfaction to receive the stream of blood that gushed from [his] victim's wounds into his mouth." Kurten committed twenty-nine murders of this sort. He was diagnosed as suffering from *haematodipsia*, literally a thirst for blood. He would strangle and cut the throats of his victims and drink their blood. He received nine death sentences.

A very famous "vampire" trial took place in England in 1949. John Haigh had murdered nine people by drinking blood from their throats. He testified in court that he had a recurrent dream of a forest in which crucifixes turned into trees that ran with blood from their branches and trunks. A man offered him a cup filled with blood, but he was always too paralyzed to take it. Each time he awoke frustrated and thirstier for blood. Finally, he slit the throat of a friend and drank the blood directly from his neck. After this, he murdered several other people, collecting their blood in glasses in order to drink it.

Living Vampires?

Clearly, there have been living vampires. To the extent that the vampires seek out and drink the blood of the living, these mass murderers all fit the definition. Whether or not early stories are based on similar murders is hard to say. But it would be an easy leap for people who already believed in vampires to think that a murderer who craved blood was a vampire. It continues to be one possible explanation.

One of the most persuasive and thorough explanations for vampires has been proposed by Paul Barber in his book *Vampires, Burial and Death* (1987). A former professor of German language and folklore, Barber believes that what sixteenth- and seventeenth-century vampire hunters found when they opened graves can be easily explained.

Barber argues that when a grave was opened, people present saw a body in a perfectly normal state of decomposition or decay. As he says, "One must learn about the reality of death and decay in order to understand the folklore of death and decay." If the vampire hunters had known what a decaying body should have looked like, they would not have been shaken by what they saw. It was their interpretation of what they saw that was wrong.

In 1591 for example, in Silesia, then part of Germany, a shoemaker committed suicide. After he was buried, several people in the village claimed

Vampire hunters prepare to open a grave and view the remains of a corpse. Fueled by ignorance, vampire hunters often attributed the normal processes of decay to vampirism.

they saw him alive and doing mischief. Town leaders dug up his grave eight months after he died to inspect it. According to their report, the body was still intact but "blown up like a drum." There was no sign of decay or stiffness. Skin on his feet had pulled away, but new skin appeared to be forming. The body did not smell. After they reburied him, people again said they saw him walking. Finally, he was exhumed again. His hands, feet, head, and heart were removed and cremated. After this, he was not seen again.

Body Decay

What are the normal processes that occur in the grave that would explain what these people saw? First, the bloating of the body is caused by a rapid growth of bacteria that produces methane gas inside the body. In some cases, the gas causes the body to expand to three times its normal size. What one sees on the mouth and other openings of the body is not fresh blood. It is frothy, liquefied tissue and decomposing blood. In time the eyes bulge, the tongue protrudes, and the face swells so that the features become grotesque. Blisters may erupt where the skin has split. The appearance of new skin is also naturally explained. "Skin slippage," or peeling, occurs in normal decomposition. What is underneath is not really new skin but looks like it.

Another vampire account provides more information to be interpreted. In Serbia in the year 1727, Arnold Paole died in an accident. Shortly before, he had revealed to his fiancee that "he had been troubled by a vampire" while in the army in Turkey. He had taken certain precautions to avoid becoming a vampire himself: he had eaten earth from the vampire's grave and had smeared himself with vampire blood. He had finally destroyed the vampire in his grave.

Despite all this, after Paole had been buried

about a month, four people in his village died. Before their deaths, they had complained of being haunted by Paole and then they had become extremely weak. His grave was opened. The district governor supervised the investigation. Paole's body seemed still fresh. His nails and skin had fallen off and been replaced by new nails and skin. His veins were full of liquid blood that had splashed all over his shroud. The people present were convinced that

A seventeenth-century tombstone. Many people claimed to have witnessed vampires rising from such graves.

"To a greater or lesser degree, vampires are photosensitive. . . . This extreme ocular photosensitivity causes their eyes to become bloodshot and subject to severe pain when exposed to the direct light of the sun."

Professor Feodor Stepanovich Andreiev, Soviet Institute of Esoteric Studies, quoted in *Vampires*

"The old tales do not say that sunlight is actively harmful to the vampire; this idea is a contribution of horror fiction and films."

Author Douglas Hill, *Man, Myth, and Magic*

Paole had indeed become a vampire. As they drove a stake through his heart, witnesses heard him give a piercing shriek, and the wound bled. They burned his body and returned the ashes into his grave.

What these witnesses experienced relates to natural body decay. In a month, the body would not appear to have decomposed very much. But on the inside, gases, decaying tissue, and blood may have caused Paole's stomach to burst, causing the stains on his shroud. What seems to be a continued growth of nails, or teeth in some accounts, is really not. It is merely the shrinking back of gums and skin. This causes the teeth and nails to appear longer than they were in life.

Paole's shriek can also be explained. According to Barber, the stake caused the swollen body to burst with the force of pent-up gases. The noise the corpse made occurs when the gases rush out past the glottis, the opening in the throat between the vocal chords. This is exactly what happens when people speak: air from the lungs vibrates the glottis, causing sound.

Shallow Graves

Other events related in vampire records include noises coming from the grave, which persuaded people that the corpse within was "undead." Barber notes how in times of plague many corpses were buried hastily, in shallow graves. The sounds of released gases or of the shifting of the body might then have been heard above ground, leading people to believe the corpse was a vampire.

Shallow graves may also have been responsible for hands or even whole bodies protruding from the earth. Rain might have eroded or washed away the soil to expose the body. Scavenging dogs or wolves might have dug up the body. These natural events would have been interpreted by peasants in terms of their own powerful belief in vampires.

Still, in some vampire records, unputrefied bodies have been dug up even a year after death. Why did these bodies not seem to decay? Barber explains that decomposition can be hastened or slowed, depending on many factors. The amount of moisture, lime, or antibiotics in the soil affects the rate of decay. How airtight the coffin is (if one is used at all) and whether the person was buried in winter or summer also affect the decay rate. Air and moisture quicken the corpse's decomposition. The presence of lime or antibiotics slows the process. In ancient Egypt, for example, the dryness of the climate and a saltlike substance called natron in the desert sand caused a natural preservation to take place and made mummification possible.

Another factor that affects the rate a body decomposes is the way a person dies. When death comes suddenly, as by murder or accident, or to a young person, decomposition is slower. It is important to notice that most vampire accounts center around people who have died in just such unusual circumstances. By digging up the graves of accident, murder or suicide victims, people would have been more likely to discover a body that fit their conception of a vampire.

Barber's insights have shed much light on the persistence of vampire belief throughout history. Noises are heard in cemeteries and superstitious people fill in the gaps with their own interpretations. Crazed and bloodthirsty murderers have made the superstition more believable. Cases of catalepsy and porphyria have certainly promoted it. Any of these might be a plausible explanation for the mystery. But even these scientific explanations cannot eliminate the mystery of the vampire. The fascination by this haunting figure continues today.

Epilogue

A tall figure is standing on the ledge immediately outside the window. . . . Intense fear paralysed the limbs of that beautiful girl. One shriek is all she can utter—with hands clasped, a face of marble, a heart beating so wildly in her bosom, that each moment it seems as if it would break its confines, eyes distended and fixed upon the window, she waits, frozen with horror. . . . She tries to scream again but a choking sensation comes over her, and she cannot. It is too dreadful—she tries to move—each limb seems wedged down by tons of lead—she can but in a hoarse faint whisper cry, —"Help—help—help!"

These lines from the 1847 novel *Varney the Vampire* conjure up the kind of scene we expect when we think about being victimized by a vampire. But this description is based on fiction, not on the actual accounts of vampire appearances.

The differences between what people think of vampires today and what ancient and medieval people thought have many explanations. For people of the past, vampires were a way to account for the unexplained—the seeming randomness of death. The world was a terrifying place to those with no scientific or rational explanations for epidemic plagues and senseless murders. As for modern people's fas-

(Opposite page) The title page of the popular *Varney the Vampire.*

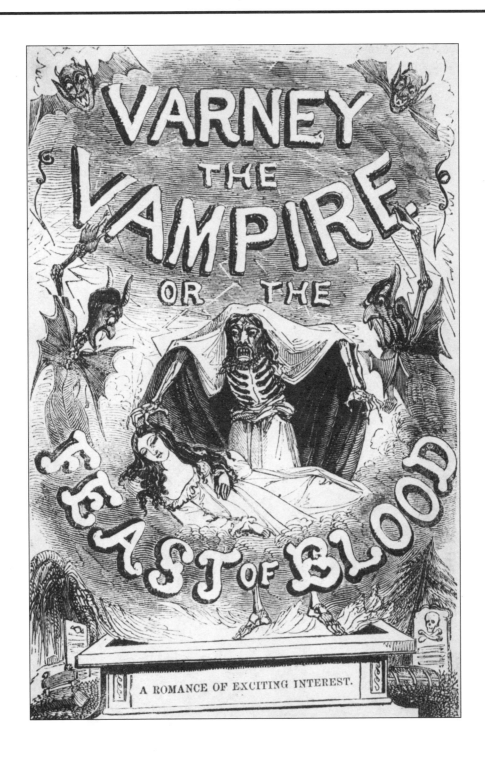

"The concept of the vampire is not only firmly rooted in legends and folk-myths of antiquity, but also established by facts of history and eye-witness accounts."

Dalhousie University professor Devendra P. Varma, *The Vampire in Legend, Lore, and Literature*

"I think it is possible to say quite firmly that vampires are not real. That is, there have never been any undead people who leave their graves at night and suck blood from the living."

Author Georgess McHargue, *Meet the Vampire*

cination with the vampire, perhaps the explanation is that vampires touch a deep psychological chord. Vampire researcher Anthony Boucher suggests that the fascination with vampires unites some common themes: "Vampirism typifies . . . that lethal alliance of love and death."

Devendra P. Varma, in her 1970 preface to *Varney the Vampire*, supplies a similar rationale, "There exists a living Dracula within us all—something ravenous, bloodsucking, and intense, something ferocious with the powers of greed, lust and violence. [The vampire] is essentially human and pathetic." Whether we read books and watch films

A still from the 1966 movie *Dracula, Prince of Darkness* with Christopher Lee. Movies like this continue to flourish. What has kept the vampire myth alive throughout history?

about vampires for these psychological reasons or simply for entertainment, each of us keeps the vampire myth alive. While we may be able to understand rationally that vampires do not exist, who among us does not start at the shadow in the window, the squeak in the dark?

For Further Exploration

Thomas G. Aylesworth, *The Story of Vampires.* New York: McGraw-Hill, 1977.

Thomas G. Aylesworth, *Vampires and Other Ghosts.* Reading, MA: Addison-Wesley, 1972.

Elwood D. Bauman, *Vampires.* New York: Watts, 1977.

Padraic Colum, *The Fountain of Youth; Stories to Be Told.* New York: The Macmillan Company, 1927.

Nancy Garden, *Vampires.* New York: Lippincott Company, 1973.

Frieda Gates, *Monsters and Ghouls: Costumes and Lore.* New York: Walker, 1980.

Giants and Ogres. Alexandria, VA: Time-Life Books, 1985.

Donald F. Glut, *The Dracula Book.* Metuchen, NJ: Scarecrow Press, 1975.

Peter Haining, ed., *The Dracula Scrapbook.* London: Bramhall House, 1976.

James W. Hinkley, *The Book of Vampires.* New York: F. Watts, 1979.

Lee Bennett Hokins, *Monsters, Ghoulies, & Creepy Creatures*. Chicago: A. Whitman, 1977.

David Pirie, *The Vampire Cinema*. New York: Crescent Books, 1977.

Lawrence P. Pringle, *Vampire Bats*. New York: Morrow, 1982.

Gabriel Ronay, *The Truth About Dracula*. New York: Stein & Day, 1972.

Leslie Shepard, ed., *The Dracula Book of Great Vampire Stories*. Secaucus, NJ: Citadel Press, 1977.

Angela Sommer-Brodenburg, *The Vampire Moves In*. New York: Dial Books for Young Readers, 1982.

Angela Sommer-Brodenburg, *The Vampire Takes a Trip*. New York: Dial Books for Young Readers, 1985.

Ian Thorne, *Dracula*. Mankato, MN: Crestwood House, 1977.

Elizabeth Warner, *Heroes, Monsters, and Other Worlds from Russian Mythology*. New York: Schocken Books, 1985.

Works Consulted

Veselin Cajkanovic, "The Killing of a Vampire," *Folklore Forum,* Vol. 7, No. 4, 1974.

Margaret Carter, ed., *Dracula: The Vampire and the Critics.* Ann Arbor, MI: M.M.I. Research Press, 1988.

Loring Danforth, *The Death Rituals of Rural Greece.* Princeton, NJ: Princeton University Press, 1982.

F. Gerard, "Transylvanian Superstitions," *The Nineteenth Century,* July 1885.

S. C. Humphreys and Helen King, eds., *Man and Immortality: The Anthropology and Archaeology of Death.* London: Academic Press, 1981.

Clive Leatherdale, *Dracula, The Novel and the Legend.* Wellingborough, Northhamptonshire, England: The Aquarian Press, 1985.

B. Demetracopolou Lee, "Greek Accounts of the Vrykolakas," *Journal of American Folklore,* Vol. 55, 1942.

Andrew Mackenzie, *Dracula Country.* London: Arthur Barker, Ltd. 1977.

Anthony Masters, *The Natural History of the*

Vampire. London: Hart-Davis, 1972.

Agnes Murgoci, "The Vampire in Roumania," *Folklore*, Vol. 37, 1926.

Felix Oinas, *Essays on Russian Folklore and Mythology*. Columbus, OH: Slavic Publishers, 1984.

Gabriel Ronay, *The Dracula Myth*. London: W. H. Allen, 1972.

Montague Summers, *The Vampire: His Kith and Kin*. London: Kegan Paul, 1928.

Montague Summers, *The Vampire in Europe*. London: Kegan Paul, 1929.

Index

About the Author

Daniel C. Scavone grew up in Chicago, Illinois. He holds a Ph.D. and is a professor of ancient and modern history at the University of Southern Indiana in Evansville. He has been awarded three National Endowment for the Humanities fellowships.

When he's not teaching, Daniel enjoys tennis, jogging, ice hockey, and singing in the Evansville Philharmonic Chorus.

Picture Credits